Space

The Sun

Charlotte Guillain

KU-711-806

www.raintreepublishers.co.uk
Visit our website to find out
more information about
Raintree books.

To order:
☎ Phone 0845 6044371
▤ Fax +44 (0) 1865 312263
▣ Email myorders@raintreepublishers.co.uk

Customers from outside the UK please telephone +44 1865 312262

Raintree is an imprint of Capstone Global Library Limited, a company incorporated in England and Wales having its registered office at 7 Pilgrim Street, London, EC4V 6LB – Registered company number: 6695582

Text © Capstone Global Library Limited 2009
First published in paperback in 2010
The moral rights of the proprietor have been asserted.

All rights reserved. No part of this publication may be reproduced in any form or by any means (including photocopying or storing it in any medium by electronic means and whether or not transiently or incidentally to some other use of this publication) without the written permission of the copyright owner, except in accordance with the provisions of the Copyright, Designs and Patents Act 1988 or under the terms of a licence issued by the Copyright Licensing Agency, Saffron House, 6–10 Kirby Street, London EC1N 8TS (www.cla.co.uk). Applications for the copyright owner's written permission should be addressed to the publisher.

Edited by Sian Smith, Rebecca Rissman, and Charlotte Guillain
Designed by Joanna Hinton-Malivoire
Picture research by Tracy Cummins and Heather Mauldin
Production by Duncan Gilbert
Originated by Heinemann Library
Printed in China

ISBN 978 0 431 02042 6 (hardback)
13 12 11 10 09
10 9 8 7 6 5 4 3 2 1

ISBN 978 1 406 26496 8 (paperback)
14 13
10 9 8 7 6 5 4

British Library Cataloguing in Publication Data
Guillain, Charlotte
   The Sun. - (Space)
   1. Sun - Juvenile literature
   I. Title
A full catalogue record for this book is available from the British Library.

Acknowledgements
We would like to thank the following for permission to reproduce photographs: Getty Images pp. 5 (©Panoramic Images), 6 (©Guy Edwardes), 7 (©Tohoku Color Agency), 9 (©Stocktrek Images), 14 (©William Radcliffe), 17 (©Smari), 18 (©DAJ), 19 (©Scott Stulberg), 22 (©Smari); NASA pp. 4, 8, 10, 23a, 23b (©SOHO); Photo Researchers Inc pp.11 (©M. Kulyk), 13 (©Roger Harris), 15 (©Detlev van Ravenswaay), 21 (©Mark Garlick); Shutterstock pp.12 (©Sebastian Kaulitzki), 20 (©Hashim Pudiyapura), 23c (©Sebastian Kaulitzki).

Front cover photograph reproduced with permission of NASA (©SOHO). Back cover photograph reproduced with permission of Shutterstock (©Sebastian Kaulitzki).

Every effort has been made to contact copyright holders of material reproduced in this book. Any omissions will be rectified in subsequent printings if notice is given to the publishers.

Contents

The Sun

The Sun is in space.

Space is up above the sky.

What is the Sun like?

The Sun is a star.

The Sun is much closer to us than
other stars.

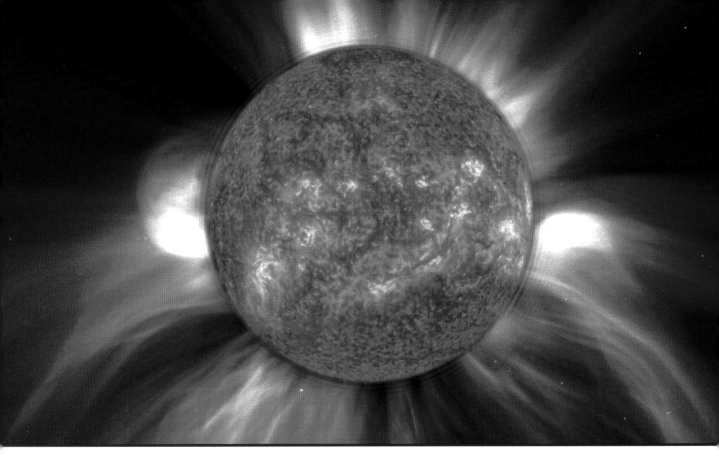

The Sun is a giant ball of gas.

The Sun is very hot and bright.

The Sun is made of layers.

centre

The Sun is hottest in the centre.

The Solar System

the Sun

The Sun and the planets around it are called the Solar System.

The planets move around, or orbit, the Sun.

The Sun gives the planets heat.

The Sun gives the planets light.

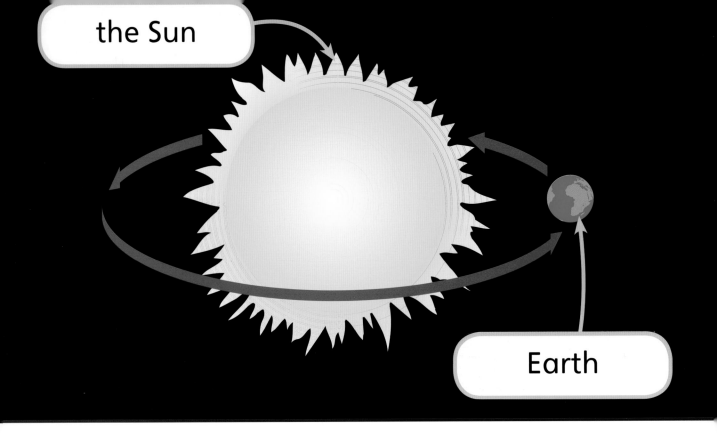

the Sun

Earth

Earth orbits the Sun.

Living things on Earth need the Sun.

The Sun gives living things light.

The Sun gives living things heat.

The Moon

The Moon does not make its own light.

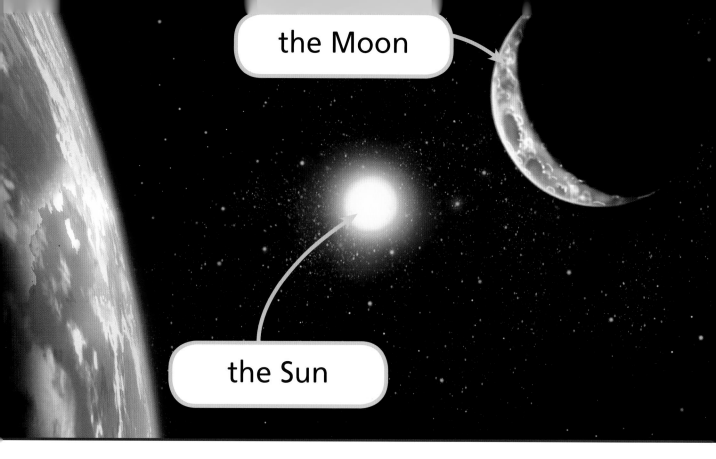

the Moon

the Sun

Light from the Sun makes the
Moon shine.

Can you remember?

Why do living things need the Sun?

22

Answer on p.24

Picture glossary

 gas not solid like wood or liquid like water. Air is a gas that we breathe in but cannot see.

 layer when something has layers it is made up of different parts that lie on top of each other

 orbit move around

 Solar System the name for the Sun and the eight planets that move around it

Index

Answer to question on p.22: Living things need the Sun for light and heat.

Notes for parents and teachers
Before reading
Ask the children what they think the Sun gives us on Earth (heat and light). Explain that the Sun is an enormous ball of extremely hot gas in the sky. We need heat and light from the Sun but we have to be careful too. Talk to the children about using sun cream and wearing a hat in sunny weather. Caution them about never looking directly at the sun.

After reading
• Make a paper plate sun. You will need a paper plate for each child. Tell them to paint the back of the plate with yellow paint. They should trace around their hand seven times. Cut out the hands and paint them yellow. Glue or staple the hands to the paper plate to make the Sun's rays.

• Make a sundial. You will need a stick approximately 30cm long. Fix the stick in the middle of an old plate using play dough. Place the stick and plate in a sunny spot in the playground. At every hour, put a small pebble to mark where the shadow of the stick falls. (Note: It may take a few days to get pebbles for each hour.) When you have a marker for each hour, talk to the children about telling the time using the sundial.